To Peggy & John
Happy Ann...
1979 Dec. 26

With love,
Billie & Al

Happy Anniversary

Happy Anniversary

The Beautiful Meanings
Of Marriage in Poetry and Prose

Selected by Barbara Kunz Loots

Hallmark Editions

The publisher wishes to thank those who have given their kind permission to reprint material included in this book. Every effort has been made to give proper acknowledgments. Any omissions or errors are deeply regretted, and the publisher, upon notification, will be pleased to make necessary corrections in subsequent editions.

Acknowledgments: Excerpt from *A Second Treasury of Kahlil Gibran.* Copyright ©1962 by The Citadel Press. Reprinted with permission of The Citadel Press. "A Good Marriage" from *To My Daughters With Love* by Pearl S. Buck. Copyright ©1967 by the Pearl S. Buck Foundation, Inc. Reprinted with permission of The John Day Company and Harold Ober Associates Incorporated. "The Precious Ingredient" from *To Marriage With Love* by Dr. David Goodman. Copyright ©1973 by Hallmark Cards, Inc. "Married Love" from *How Love Grows in Marriage* by Leland Foster Wood. Copyright 1950 by Leland Foster Wood. Reprinted by permission of Hawthorn Books, Inc. Excerpt from *The Taste of New Wine* by Keith Miller. Copyright ©1965 by Keith Miller. Reprinted by permission of the publisher, Word Books. "Down Life's Highway" from *The Gypsy Heart* by Emily Carey Alleman. Copyright 1957 by Emily Carey Alleman. Reprinted by arrangement. "Hour of Night" by Esther York Burkholder. Copyright 1953 by Esther York Burkholder. Reprinted by arrangement. "Perspective" by Anne Campbell. Reprinted by permission of the author. "Milestones" by Louise Hajek from *The Chicago Tribune.* Reprinted by permission. "Anniversary" by Betty Isler from *Saturday Evening Post.* Reprinted by arrangement. "Quiet Evening" by Gladys McKee. First published in *Radio Mirror.* Reprinted by permission of the author.

Love joins our present
with the past and the future.

Kahlil Gibran

Circle of Love

I wrote your name within my heart
Then wrote my name below
And drew a circle round about
So many years ago.
We placed our circles' endless love
Within two shining bands of gold
And sealed our love with kisses then,
With words, "to have and hold."
And as we celebrate each year,
Our love enriched and grown,
I hold your heart encircled still
For you are mine,
     my own!

Lenore Link

Enduring Treasures

Love views each day
with eager eyes...
with wonder and surprise,
with fresh delight
in simple pleasures.
   Love dreams its dreams
   and dries its tears
   and through the busy years
   gathers bright,
   enduring treasures.

Barbara Burrow

Perspective

I think when we grow old together
And we look backward down the years,
On rainy days and sunny weather,
And mingled smiles and tears;

The mountain peak of every sorrow
That casts a somber shadow still,
When viewed upon that far tomorrow
Will seem a little hill.

And you will touch my hand with meaning,
And I shall smile a russet smile,
And we shall whisper, closer leaning,
"The venture was worthwhile!"

Anne Campbell

We Two

We two make home of any place we go;
We two find joy in any kind of weather;
Or if the earth is clothed in bloom or snow,
If summer days invite, or bleak winds blow,
What matters it if we two are together?
We two, we two, we make our world, our weather.

Ella Wheeler Wilcox

Mature Love

This wonderful love of maturity makes the lovely fires of youth pale beside its magnificence; its rich and warmer glow; its fruits of experience which only add charm and beauty to the mystery of love; its trust in each other and the deeper understanding of intimate and cherished moments which no sorrow can blot out....

Sylvia Gray

The Bond of Marriage

The divinest gift of marriage is this—the daily, unconscious growing of two souls into one. Aspirations and ambitions merge, each with the other, and love grows fast to love. Unselfishness answers to unselfishness, tenderness responds to tenderness, and the highest joy of each is the well-being of the other. The words of Church and State are only the seal of a predestined compact. Day by day and year by year the bond becomes closer and dearer, until at last the two are one, and even death is no division.

Myrtle Reed

Anniversary

Had someone told me
    twenty years ago
That I could love you more
    than on that day,
I would have laughed and
    said, "It is not so,"
And gone sure-heartedly
    along my way.
But now the brook in ever-
    deepening flow
Has carved our lives, as
    pebbles in the sand
Turned ceaselessly by
    currents to and fro,

This way and that; so have
    you held my hand
Through all vicissitudes,
    throughout the slow
Maturing years, through
    darkened hours of pain.
Thus, as the colors of the
    pebbles show
Their richness in the depths,
    so does love gain.
Had someone told me
    twenty years ago....
But then I did not know, I
    did not know.

                    Betty Isler

Milestones

To me it seems that stars will ever be
Bright markers on the road of memory.
For I remember stars like silver flame
That magic night when you first spoke my name.
A cloak of evening stars then seemed to fall
Just like a benediction over all.
And when I looked for love, to my surprise
I found the answer in your star-filled eyes.

Louise Hajek

Hour of Night

We have come home and closed the door
After an evening city-bright,
Home to familiar wall and floor.
Let us turn out each light,
Saving one quiet hour more
To know the night.

Draw back the curtain. Let a star,
A hill and pine tree tell us why
The heart-deep satisfactions are
A spot of earth, a square of sky,
A full moon only treetop-far
And you and I.

Esther York Burkholder

When Love Says Most

Love's in the merest look, the lightest touch,
The thought almost too subtle to recall;
When love is deepest, words may be too much.
True lovers do not need a sign at all;
They have, and do not even have to reach.
When love says most, it has least need of speech.

James Dillet Freeman

A Good Marriage

A good marriage is one where love is not destroyed. Love changes, of course, in its manifestation as time goes on and as individuals achieve higher levels of maturity, but change does not mean destruction. It can and should mean growth. A good marriage is one which allows for change and growth in the individuals and in the way they express their love.

Pearl S. Buck

The Precious Ingredient

It is good to know that you are loved just as you are. Instinctively you feel grateful to the one who so loves you that he will accept and endure the weaknesses which beset you and which you have not yet learned to overcome. Life is peaceful and pleasant on this basis....

Love is an art. Marriage is an art. The art of love in marriage can be learned. But all the time we must keep in mind that the precious ingredient in our marriage is love.

Dr. David Goodman

Two people unselfish and considerate,
tactful and warmhearted,
and salted with humor, who are
in love, have the most essential
of all qualifications for a
successful marriage—they have character.

William Lyon Phelps

The Colors of Love

New love is pink, blush.
        The whole world looks bright
When seen through
        The rose glow of delight.

Love is orange-yellow,
        Warm as the sun,
Radiant, vital,
        When two are as one.

Blue is regret
        For the words left unspoken,
Kindness forgotten,
        Promises broken.

Pure white is the love
That comforts, that cares,
Forgetful of self,
All burdens bears.

Gold are the memories,
Golden the laughter,
Golden forgiveness
And grace ever after.

Happiness, sadness,
Peacefulness, strife—
The colors of love
Are the colors of life.

Ruth A. Jacob

There is an inner life in a marriage—a life
which is lived out when two marriage partners
are together with no one else present.
This private relationship I shall call
the soul of a marriage....The soul
of a marriage can be a trysting place
where two people can come together quietly
from the struggles of the world
and feel safe, accepted, and loved....

Keith Miller

Quiet Evening

What is there in the evening
When children are in bed
That waits to be spoken,
That wants to be said,
Above soft, muted music,
In the circled gold
Of lamplight and starlight
What needs to be told?
The knowing heart can answer,
Keeping as it goes
Love's daily record
Of the thorn, the rose;
But the lips that would tell it
Are silent and wise,
And the words are spoken
Only by the eyes,
And your hand touching softly
Upon my cheek, my hair,
And the silken sound of quiet
Upon the evening air.

Gladys McKee

We're Fun Together

We're fun together
   because we share.
We share late night movies,
   Sunday morning coffee,
      special songs,
      private jokes,
      and each other.
We solve problems by dividing
and our happiness multiplies.
We're fun together
   because we share love.

Robin St. John

The Happiest Moment

If I could go back in time
And relive the happiest moment of my life,
What hour would I choose?
Perhaps the day when I became your wife?
Or would my choice go farther yet
To that bright day when we first met?
So many choices would be mine—
Little thoughtful times you've given me,
The unexpected joys we shared,
A special anniversary.
But Dear, I think if I could choose
From all the happy times I've known with you
I'd pass them all and take tomorrow,
For as our marriage grows,
    my joy keeps growing, too.

Mary Dawson Hughes

Together

We have made a home...
a place to share
our comforts
and treasures...
a shelter
from life's disappointments...
a place where joy and laughter
are always welcome.
Together we have made a home...
a home for love.

Mark Geppert

The Couple in the Photo

They seem so unposed,
   so easy in their love.
      Note:
   his protective arm,
   her contented smile.
It's as though they couldn't imagine
   being anywhere
      but together.
   Beautiful, don't you think,
   that after all this time
   those two happy people
      are still
      us.

Edward Cunningham

What Is Love?

LOVE is not just looking at each other and saying, "You're wonderful." There are times when we are anything but wonderful....

LOVE is looking outward together in the same direction. It is linking our strength to pull a common load. It is pushing together towards the far horizons, hand in hand.

LOVE is knowing that when our strength falters, we can borrow the strength of someone who cares.

LOVE is a strange awareness that our sorrows will be shared and made lighter by sharing; that joys will be enriched and multiplied by the joy of another.

LOVE is knowing someone else cares, that we are not alone in life.

LOVE is of God, for God is love. When we love, we touch the hem of the garment of God.

Patrick Scanlon

A Patient Love

I do not envy
The young lovers
Their frantic urgency
Their impatience
Their instant
Everything

I hold precious
The slow evolving
Of a rooted love
Willing to wait
The unforced blossom.

Betty Isler

My Quiet Place

The world
    keeps spinning, spinning,
    and the days
    go rushing by,
    and sometimes
    there is scarcely time
    to stop
    and wonder why...
But, inside me,
    there's a quiet place
    where hope and faith renew,
    where the world, the world
    can't reach me...
That quiet place is you.

Francee Davis

Remembering

My memory book is in my mind. No scrapbook could ever hold the laughter we shared on that spring morning or the warm kiss that began our married life so long ago. Memories of the years we've seen, the good times when we gave each other joy, the bad times when we gave each other strength—are all stored safely. No need to turn pages or search in drawers. Our memories are a part of me as your love is, dear. And I cherish both deep within my heart.

Tina Hacker

Married Love

Married living needs the continuance of the dash and sparkle of romantic love. But the relation of romantic love to married love is somewhat like that of a little tree to the larger tree which it later becomes. It has life and fresh young energy that enables it to grow. When it has grown into a larger tree its heart and vitality are still there but, with continued life, it has taken new rings of growth, its branches have spread wider and its roots have gone deeper. Moreover it bears flowers and fruit which the little tree did not produce.

Married love is love woven into a pattern of living. It has in it the elements of understanding and of the passionate kindness of husband and wife toward each other. It is rich in the many-sided joys of life because each is more concerned with giving joy than with grasping it for himself. And joys are most truly experienced when they are most fully shared.

Leland Foster Wood

Now and Then

How filled with seductive charms
Love in young fashion is.
But be glad that even old arms
Embrace love, longer than beauty,
Longer than passion is.

Barbara Kunz Loots

Hold These Things Dear

Hold these things dear for me—
That once, just yesterday, you said,
"I'll share my life with you,
Whatever lies ahead."
Hold these things dear for me—
That through the passing years
Somehow the strength we've found
    and shared
Has vanquished all the fears.
And, somehow, in a world that spins
At an ever faster pace,
We still can find a pleasant world
In a loving, shared embrace.

Kensinger Jones

$\mathcal{L}$ove puts the beauty
in everyday things—
the comfort in a touch,
the music in a word,
the warmth in a home,
the joy in a memory,
the "we" in a dream.

Karen Ravn

Down Life's Highway

Hand in hand, together,
    Traveling life's highway;
We find the journey pleasant,
    Sharing day by day.

Sharing the sweet and the bitter,
    Sharing the pleasure and pain,
We take the sun with the shadow,
    Laugh at the silver rain.

Laugh at the storms and brave them,
    Seeking to understand;
We find the fruit of life sweeter,
    Traveling hand in hand.

Emily Carey Alleman

Second Honeymoon

Remember our first honeymoon?
The wine we drank was new for we were young,
And any wine seemed bright upon the tongue;
Now we are connoisseurs by right of years,
By right of laughter shared and mingled tears;
This mellow wine is fire to the taste,
The dusty bottle savoured not in haste,
But vintage wine we raise in gallant toast
To second honeymoons, and Time, our host.

Bessie F. Collins

An anniversary toast
to precious moments present,
to precious moments past,
to precious moments yet to come
and to a love that will always last.

Jack Mason

Set in Romanee, a twentieth-century typeface designed by Jan van Krimpen of Holland.
Printed on Hallmark Crown Royale Book paper.
Designed by Lilian Weytjens.